JOE'S GIFT

Joseph Alff, M.S.W.

PRESS

Joe's Gift
by Joseph Alff, M.S.W.

Printed in the United States of America

ISBN 9781628391626

www.xulonpress.com

Cover painting by Erica Chappuis

Books by Joseph Alff

*THE SECRET TO LIVING A MORE
FULFILLED LIFE
JOE'S GIFT*
Available at Amazon.com and on Kindle, Barnes
& Noble (BN.com) and Xulonpress.com/bookstore
— 866-909-book(2665)

To Jen and Chris,
with love

ACKNOWLEDGEMENTS

I can't thank Mike Denomme, Sara Devine, Keith Mitchell and Roy Barnes enough for their support, understanding and keen insights as I struggled with writing this book. At one time or another each of them provided just the right words of encouragement, thoughtful comments and/or editorial corrections that were spot on.

Special thanks to Ken Eatherly, whose superb editing once again clarified and polished my writing considerably.

What superlatives can I use to describe artist Erica Chappuis and her outstanding cover design? She understood the essence of this book better than I did.

Thanks to Tim Fox, who encouraged me to write another book every time we met.

And to my wife, Marge, who didn't question my sanity for wanting to venture into these tricky writing waters again.

FOREWORD

At some point on life's journey to discover meaning and truth each person has to learn the difference between profundity and complexity and, as a corollary, the difference between what is simple and what is simplistic. The famous Swiss Protestant theologian Karl Barth knew the difference. The story goes that he had just concluded a lecture on an American university campus, when one student came up to him and expressed concern that the depth and subtlety of the great man's thought had left him bewildered. Of the many summaries of the exchange, this is the one I prefer: "Isn't there some way," the student asked, "that you could capture in a sentence the essence of your thought?" "Yes there is," replied Barth. "All you need to know is expressed in these simple words from the Sunday school song: 'Jesus loves me, this I know, for the Bible tells me so.'" But the eminent Catholic theologian, Thomas Aquinas, may have done Barth one better: Toward the end of his life, the saintly priest had such a profound experience of mystical union that he pronounced his many works "so much straw" in comparison with what he had just encountered. The Angelic Doctor never wrote another word.

It goes without saying that Joe Alff has not created a voluminous body of complex thought in the manner of these immensely influential theologians. And he certainly would never pretend to be even remotely in their class when it comes to theological sophistication. If Joe does not share with these great scholars impressive tomes of theoretical analysis, however, he does share with them an invaluable quality. Like these sages before him, Joe has acquired the rare ability to see through the clutter of life all around him and discern what is truly important. In short, he knows a simple, profound truth when he sees one.

A voracious reader and an inquisitive thinker, Joe has spent decades probing the great issues of our time. Take it from someone who has spent many an evening with him at our favorite bistro, nursing a beer or two: This is a man who refuses to embrace simplistic solutions to life's challenging questions. Readers of Joe's first book, **The Secret to Living a More Fulfilled Life**, know full well that he will not hesitate to challenge the accepted spiritual wisdom of American culture. At the conclusion of this first work, Joe resoundingly affirmed the critical importance of humility and contrition, two concepts that hardly come tripping off the tongue when one thinks of the classic American prescription for living a happier, more meaningful life. Joe is certainly not one given to offering the warm and fuzzy comfort that he believes far too often underpins the sugary spiritual commentary that many Americans embrace.

What, then, can readers expect from this new work, which the author has simply called **Joe's Gift**? They can expect an amazing journey through the many intriguing gateways that the virtue of humility takes them. As I have indicated, it is a virtue that assumed paramount importance in Joe's prescription for a more fulfilled life. In **Joe's Gift** he takes humility and gives it the kind of insightful, multidimensional analysis that reveals its rightful role as the key to spiritual development. With humility serving as a guiding light, Joe brings his readers to journey's end: the secret to his gift. And it will also bring us back to the truth that the stories of our two eminent theologians had so poignantly revealed. Ultimately, it is precisely Joe's hardboiled credibility as one who refuses to settle for comforting views of human nature and of the human condition that makes his conclusion so powerful and, yes, so surprising. What Joe discovers has always been there in plain view for him and for all of us to see. It is there that Joe's gift wondrously becomes our own.

Michael Denomme, Ph.D.

St. John, who was Jesus' beloved apostle, was supposedly known for delivering the same short sermon, regardless of the occasion or circumstances: "Brothers and sisters, love one another." When members of his congregation asked whether they couldn't, sometime, hear a different message, he answered: "When you have mastered this lesson, we can move on to another."

Robert Ellsberg, *All Saints*

When I die, just keep playing the records.

Jimi Hendrix

I can't remember what I thought or said when a college classmate made the comment to me. It, however, threw me for a loop. I have thought about it for decades, wondering what my reply should have been.

"Joe," he said, "the problem with you is that everything you do is average."

Man, what do you say to that!

I suppose it could have been worse. He could have described me as being below average in everything I do.

It's a disturbing thought — being average. Possessing nothing distinctive. Living, by inference, a ho-hum, ordinary and relatively meaningless existence.

I have repeated this comment to a number of friends over the years; hoping, I suppose, that they would provide me solace by refuting it. They instead had little to say in response, suggesting to me that they agreed with it.

They might also have been silently considering if the comment applied to them; wondering if their lives are no more than average and ordinary.

Most people respond to this issue by simply sweeping it under the carpet and dancing over it. This may indeed be the best response. Why ruminate on it? It's just a lot of semantics. Take each day by the horns and live life to the fullest, whether that fullest is average or not.

I wish I could do that, but I can't. I needed to look this issue in the eye and come to some resolution.

The question became for me: What is my gift to the world? What is "Joe's Gift?" What is anyone's gift to the world?

If I'm ordinary, as my classmate averred, then how can I, or anyone for that matter, become extraordinary?

Or as Marlon Brando playing Terry Malloy in the movie, *On The Waterfront*, tragically states, "I could have been 'a somebody'."

How does anyone become "a somebody?"

This short book describes how I came to an answer that finally satisfied me.

I was once on the phone with a friend. He had to leave the phone to do something. When he returned, he apologized for taking so long, stating that he had to walk past a mirror!

I remember a work session with a colleague in a room that had a wall of mirrors. We didn't get much done as he kept viewing himself in the mirrors. I half expected him to address the mirror: "Mirror, mirror on the wall, who's the fairest one of all?"

That, sadly, is how most of us function: We spend much of our time looking at ourselves and failing to see the world around us. Instead of looking through clear glass that allows us to see and interact with our surroundings, we keep looking in mirrors that reflect only our needs, wants, experiences and opinions with barely a sense or appreciation of what is happening around us.

It's egotism that keeps us trapped in an average, ordinary world. If we wish to be extraordinary and special, to bless the world with our gift, we must start the process by breaking out of this totally self-centered existence.

As Jesus said, "Why do you look at the speck of sawdust in your brother's eye and pay no attention to the plank in your own eye?" Matthew 7:3

I could have easily become defensive, and then offensive, when my classmate made the comment. I could have said, "Well, you're not so hot yourself." Or I could have followed a friend's advice and said, "How would you like a better-than-average punch in the mouth?"

No. I had to address this issue, wherever it took me sans self-justifications, rationalizations and even anger. It called for a candid and honest understanding of who I am by looking through clear glass and not at mirrors.

I needed the courage shown by a soldier I knew in the Army. He had entered Officers Candidate School. I thought that would be the last I would see of him, yet a few months later he showed up back in the unit. I asked him what happened. He replied, "I wasn't good enough to be an Army officer."

How often do you hear that kind of honesty?

I still think he would make an outstanding Army officer.

But alas, as a mental health counselor for almost 40 years, and a practiced observer of human behavior, I am aware of the narrow worlds I and others live in.

Decades ago I watched an episode on the *Candid Camera* TV show where an enclosure was built around a woman who was playing a slot machine. She was oblivious to the sawing, hammering and commotion all around her.

There was an episode on the popular TV show, *The Office*, where the office staff seeks to prove that Stanley is unaware of his surroundings. Stanley is frequently shown doing crossword puzzles and rolling his eyes during staff meetings. His co-workers dress up in outrageous outfits and keep passing by Stanley. Stanley gives no evidence that he sees any of them.

I have traveled with a number of people in a car who talked, talked, talked. There was no let up. We could pass the most interesting or beautiful sight and the chatty passengers never noticed. They are like children traveling in the family van and watching DVDs. They are transfixed. It keeps the youngsters quiet, yet they are oblivious to anything outside.

I remember seeing an ad years ago showing a minivan with two children in the back seats watching a video. It is parked in a national park with a panoramic view of majestic mountains. The ad was meant to sell potential buyers on the vehicle's video system.

I thought to myself when I saw this ad that the parents drove all that way for their children to enjoy the Great Outdoors and the kids are glued to some Bugs Bunny video.

Teenagers often seem to be oblivious to their environment. The library in our town is down the street from the high school. On a few occasions I have attempted to pull out of the library's parking lot onto the street crowded with drivers leaving school. It's a difficult task. I sit there waiting for a teen driver to notice me and allow me to enter the line of cars. It takes a while.

They don't notice me. They don't notice much of anything going on around them. They are in another world, preoccupied with other things. Is it any wonder that car insurance rates for teenage drivers are so high.

Ah, but people protest that they do see what's happening around them. But do they?

There is a scene in the TV drama, *The Wire*. A police department head is interviewing an officer who wants a job in his group. At the end of the interview the department head asks the applicant to describe exactly where the building he entered is and where he is in the building (e.g. The building is located at the southwest corner of Main and Broadway and I'm currently on the north side of the building, on the third floor in room 306). The applicant flubbed his answer and was passed over.

This is the question Sherlock Holmes brought before his faithful companion Watson in "A Scandal in Bohemia." Holmes is instructing Watson on the difference between seeing and observing.

"You see, but you do not observe. The distinction is clear. For example, you have frequently seen the steps which lead up from the hall to this room."

"Frequently."

"How often?"

"Well, some hundreds of times."

"Then how many are there?"

"How many? I don't know."

"Quite so! You have not observed. And yet you have seen. That is just my point. Now, I know there are seventeen steps, because I have both seen and observed."

People see but they don't observe.

Years ago I occasionally gave a lecture on couples' relationships. I usually began by asking the participants a number of questions about their spouses. The questions included:

Name your spouse's two closest friends.

What did he or she wear yesterday?

Describe in detail what he or she did yesterday.

What is his or her favorite meal?

What is one of his or her favorite movies?

Name one of his or her concerns or worries.

Name one of his or her major rivals or enemies.

What medical problem does he or she worry about?

Of all the people you both know, who does he or she like the least?

Name one of his or her favorite novels, TV shows, sports.

Most class members were surprised, even embarrassed, by how little they knew about their spouses, even though they might have been together for decades.

How can a person see and observe? How can we throw off the mirrors that imprison us and replace them with clear glass that liberates us and expands our world?

I recently read a true crime story about a British woman who was murdered in Tokyo. A reporter was covering the case. He began to suspect that someone was following him and possibly wanted to harm him. He reported his concerns to the police. They advised him to keep a sharp lookout for anyone who might be following him. He did just that: looking closely at everyone around him to determine if anyone evidenced ill-intentions toward him. He said he was amazed how much he learned about his environment. He saw people and things he never saw before. The world around him opened up.

As a mental health consultant for Head Start programs, I had to go to various schools throughout Detroit. The company I worked for periodically had police officers address the staff on how to avoid getting mugged while working. They stated that the typical mugger's MO is to sneak up behind the victim, tell them not to turn around, take his or her money, and flee unnoticed. They don't want to be seen.

Muggers target "space cadets," that is, people who are walking around with their heads in the clouds, unaware of what is going on around them.

You greatly lessen your chances of getting mugged by being actively aware of your environment. This means observing the parking lot as you enter it. If anything looks suspicious, drive on. If you see a suspicious person, look that person in the eye. He will know you have seen him and he will move on.

The number one way to avoid being involved in a car accident is being aware of your environment.

Don't just look at the other drivers: Anticipate what they might or might not do next.

Decades ago I saw TV coverage of the pope moving through a crowd. He was intensely scanning virtually every face. I learned afterward that he always does this: He is looking for Jesus.

Camera bugs are always scanning the world around them for interesting shots. Detectives scrutinize a crime scene for clues. Birdwatchers are alert to every sight and sound in the wild.

Writers are very attuned to their environment. I am constantly scanning my environment for things to put into my books that others might overlook.

If people don't see much of the world around them, they are listening to even less.

From my years as a psychiatric counselor, I will never forget Dave and Diane. They were a married couple with two pre-teen boys. It would be incorrect to label the one-hour weekly sessions I had with them as marital counseling. They were more like the no-holds-barred cage matches seen on TV, though thankfully no physical blows were exchanged. The blows were all emotional and psychological.

The sessions would begin calmly enough, until one would hurl an accusation at the other, who would in turn hurl one back. They were then off to the races: Screaming at each other until one of them would either clam up or bolt from the office. I was more a referee than a counselor.

As you can guess, nothing constructive came from these sessions.

Following my father's death, my mother bought a duplex in Buffalo. She lived in the upper unit while she rented out the lower unit over the years. One tenant was a family consisting of the parents and their two teenage daughters. They seemed to have one mode of communication: screaming at each other. I couldn't imagine how my mother endured hearing all that screaming day in and day out. She was a very placid and reserved person.

The father owned a Buick on which he lavished great care and attention. I often thought he would be a much happier person if he put as much care and attention into his family as he did his car.

Family strife occurs at all levels. My wife, Marge, and I have a friend who has been feuding with his siblings in order to protect his father's estate. His sister once called him at work and cussed him out royally. He now isn't talking to them.

A friend of mine ended up communicating with his sister-in-law via certified letters concerning his mother's estate.

A frightful example of "locking horns," as the expression goes, is an exhibit in the Maine State Museum. Two exhumed moose bulls were found deadlocked in battle, their antlers inseparably stuck together. It appears that the more they fought, the more entangled they became until both dropped dead from exhaustion.

Now that's being bullheaded!

Welcome to the world of marital, family and personal conflicts where the constant fighting ensnares both persons till they drop from exhaustion and the relationship dies.

This sad beat occurs everywhere, even in churches where love is supposed to prevail.

Years ago I was on a church search committee to find a new rector. At the start, all was harmony. We agreed we would work till we found a candidate acceptable to all committee members, and by inference, to all church members. Those good intentions soon collapsed as theologically liberal and conservative groups formed, espousing their preferred candidate. Each side continually made their case for their candidate. The other side dutifully listened and silently disregarded everything that was said.

Both camps were dug in, unwilling to give an inch. It got so bad, I humorously noted that if one side brought in a police rap sheet showing that the candidate favored by the other side had been molesting children for decades, it would have been dismissed as being irrelevant.

The final vote ran down "party lines." But battles are rarely over at the end of a war. This one wasn't. Painful repercussions reverberated throughout the parish for years to come.

We have two very politically minded friends, one a liberal Democrat and the other a very conservative Republican. They frequently "discuss" political issues verbally and through emails. They don't scream at each other, but their communications are more like ping-pong games where each person is slamming the ball to make the winning point. The other person slams the ball back harder. Neither is changing their views one iota.

Marge and I have both Democrat and Republican friends and are around people in both parties. Both factions tend to clump together, happily stating their political convictions by preaching to the choir, which reinforces in their minds the validity of their views. A few don't even like being around people with opposing political views, dismissing them as being ill-informed or just plain dumb.

Whenever people are "making their case" for something, I'm reminded of the country-western song sung by the Time Jumpers titled, *Three Sides to Every Story,* that says, *There are three sides to every story: your side ... my side ... and the truth.*

To find the truth, people must *listen-to-learn,* however difficult that can be.

Listening-to-learn involves asking good questions. It also involves restating what the speaker said, to the speaker's satisfaction; e.g., "You feel I ignore you when I ... Is this correct?"

Years ago two friends visited with Marge and me after attending a weekend family gathering. They came all the way from Maine to Michigan for the event. They were hurt and angry when they told us that, during those two days, not a single family member asked them about their life in Maine.

Marge once gave me a T-shirt that had a picture of a book on it with the inscription, "Ask Me About My Book." It usually draws laughs when I wear it, probably because it speaks a truth. People rarely ask about things that are important to us. Maybe we should all wear a sign with the inscription, "Ask Me About _____ (fill in the blank)."

There is a political adage that says politicians should answer the question they *want* asked rather than the question that *is* asked. That really is what most people do in conversations. They steer the conversation in the direction of what's important to them.

I once joked with my son that I was writing an article titled, "Twelve ways to work into any conversation that my son is attending Harvard Business School."

It's a wonder that anything meaningful gets exchanged through human communications when all most people are doing is impatiently waiting for "air time."

Some people simply circle their wagons and won't let any new ideas or practices penetrate their defenses.

Over the years I have invited any number of friends to attend Sunday service with us, especially on Easter Sunday when the service is especially beautiful and joyous. I assure them that this is a one-time-only deal: I won't ask them to attend another service. Almost all refuse. It's like they are Christian church phobic. Their blind resistance makes no sense to me.

I also know people who won't budge from their position that unless a person accepts Jesus Christ as their savior they are eternally doomed. The thought that a Muslim's prayers are pleasing to God isn't on their radar screens.

These people are like our children who would refuse to eat something new, proclaiming that they don't like it before even tasting it. As I used to tell them, "Try it, you might like it."

I was speaking to a church parishioner about another member who is squandering his considerable talents to alcohol, drugs and womanizing. We wondered what will save him from his demons.

He said something that intrigued me. "Nathan," he said, "needs to open his heart."

I later wondered: What does it mean to open your heart?

I suspect it begins with being humble. It's humility that breaks down those self-centering mirrors, which then allows us to live fuller, richer lives.

But what does it mean to be humble? It's a word that gets tossed around a lot yet there is little consensus as to what it actually means or how it should be practiced.

Trying to figure out what exactly humility is, I have found, is very humbling.

In my book, *The Secret to Living a More Fulfilled Life*, the secret is contrition and humility. People who responded to the book picked up on various things they liked in it but virtually no one said a word about contrition and humility.

I suspect this was because most people misunderstand the meaning of humility. (Note: I will combine contrition and humility hereafter as humility.)

My son, Chris, was working for a business consulting firm at the time of the release of my first book. He broached the topic of humility and its usefulness in the business world to some colleagues. They deemed it counterproductive and potentially career-destroying. I suspect that to the business-oriented mind humble people are pushovers and pushovers get squashed in the business world.

Before retiring my friend Fred ran a company that developed and managed senior cooperative housing. He said that admitting wrongdoing even when it's true frequently results in a rat's nest of legal problems; but, he added, there are ways of admitting mistakes without inflicting too much damage to the company.

But the primary complaint against living a humble life rests in the belief that it's a huge downer. Life is hard enough, these people reason, so why add to its burdens by beating up on yourself, which they assume humility is all about.

But are such negative views of humility valid?

Humility, I have found, has many surprising faces.

There's a story that George Washington Carver, the ex-slave and award-winning, pioneering botanist, grew frustrated in his efforts to unlock the secrets of nature through his experiments. He turned to God for help, asking him to at least reveal the secrets of the lowly peanut to him.

Carver went on to develop a hundred uses derived from peanuts, including cosmetics, dyes, plastics, gasoline and nitroglycerin.

In the 1950's I enjoyed watching the TV show *You Bet Your Life* with Groucho Marx. During one episode Groucho asked a contestant what he did for a living. The contestant said he is buying up all the land he can get between Los Angeles and San Diego. Groucho looked at him like he was crazy and asked him why he would do something so foolish. The contestant just smiled and said if there is anyone watching the show who owns land between Los Angeles and San Diego he would like to talk with them.

Dan Gilbert, the billionaire chairman and founder of Quicken Loans, Inc., has over the past few years purchased or controls over 30 office and residential buildings in downtown Detroit, to the amazement of practically everyone who has written off Detroit. But as one local TV reporter said, "Where others see empty buildings, Dan Gilbert sees opportunities."

I knew a retired auto executive who once told me that throughout his career he never backed off from tasks that were below his skill level. He, in fact, gladly undertook these tasks and addressed them as if they were the most important tasks in the company. His thoroughness with "unimportant" things invariably led to better things for him and for the company.

My friend Rich from our church told me he initially rejected the rector's request that he head up the children's ministry, thinking it was an insult to his skills. He should be teaching adults, not children. Yet he swallowed his pride and accepted the assignment. He discovered he has a gift for teaching children and now cherishes these classes.

When I was unemployed I took any professionally related job that came my way. Many of them were for only a couple hours a week. Some, like grief counseling at funeral homes, and leading a diabetes support group, were unfamiliar to me yet I jumped into them. I took a position as a mental health consultant for Head Start Programs for four hours a week. That piddling job turned into very rewarding full-time work not long afterward.

Small, seemingly insignificant things that turned into grand things.

When others under him made mistakes that led to national policy disasters, Abraham Lincoln always said the fault lay with him. These humble acts of forgiveness resulted in subordinates who then worked even harder for the President.

My friend Tim has had a very successful career developing and managing senior citizen and family-oriented housing complexes. He once proposed to his partner that they end their relationship. He offered the partner his choice of the properties to be divided, which he did, and they then went their separate ways. Tim continued to grow his business and to prosper "beyond anything I ever imagined."

Abraham and his nephew Lot parted in similar fashion as recorded in the Book of Genesis, chapter 13. Abraham offered Lot his choice of land. Lot choose the verdant area, and they went their separate ways. Abraham then prospered while Lot floundered.

Bruce Burton was the owner and president of Burtek, a successful and growing manufacturing company before selling it a few years ago. He once told me he is very mindful of his behavior and of the business decisions he makes knowing they will impact some 425 families who depend on him for their daily needs. He writes, "The reality of responsibility would sink in at the company picnics where we had almost 1,000 people there and I thought, 'I am responsible for every mortgage payment here.' "

I learned of an incredible example of humble behavior decades ago while I was participating in a renewal weekend at a Detroit catholic church. I was leading a discussion group when suddenly a church parishioner stormed into the room, sat down and informed me and the group that he didn't appreciate these Protestants coming to his church and telling them what they should believe. He then stormed out.

I mentioned the incident the next morning to one of the parish priests who was in the group. He told me that Tony is an interesting fellow. He holds strong opinions and frequently voices them. He said when the Vatican decreed that Catholic churches must move the altar from the head of the sanctuary to the middle of the church, Tony loudly protested the move, calling it a desecration. Yet when the church decided to comply with the order, Tony wrote a check for the move and was there to help move the altar.

I once read about a person who was visiting someone in his home. He noticed a portrait of the current president hanging on the wall. He found this surprising because the president belonged to a different political party than did the homeowner. He asked the homeowner why he would display a portrait of the president when he didn't agree with his politics. The homeowner answered, "Because he's our president."

So we have three individuals who were dismissed for investing in things no one else wanted — the lowly peanut, a lot of "useless land" in southern California, and empty buildings in downtown Detroit; three individuals who gladly performed "lowly tasks;" another individual who took the blame when others made mistakes; two persons who let others get the better part of deals; another person who took his responsibility toward his employees and their families to heart, and two very humble individuals who put their personal beliefs aside and supported the will of the majority.

All humble attitudes and acts.

So what is the essence of humility? What is its definition?

My friend Sara Devine writes, "I see humility as compassion, kindness, respect and deference. When I think of "humble" people, I think of the Dalai Lama, Nelson Mandela, Gandhi, Martin Luther King, and Bishop Tutu, to name a few. However, I'm not sure these great men were meek, nor submissive. It's a bit of a conundrum (a riddle). I'd like to ponder it further."

I advised Sara not to ponder it any further since finding a definition for humility is akin to nailing

Jell-O to the wall: It's nearly impossible to do. Humility is simply one of those you'll-know-it-when-you-see-it things.

Instead of trying to define humility, let us explore how it opens up the world around us.

Humility Opens Our Eyes and Ears:

STOP-LOOK-LISTEN

Quit the constant yakking, take a break from always clicking pictures, shut off the cell phone and open your senses to the world around you.

"Be still, and know that I am God." Psalms 46:10

Marge and I visited a number of national parks in the American Southwest years ago. We stayed in cabins in the parks. There were no phones, TVs, Wi-Fi or radios in the cabins. It forced us to take in the sights, sounds and smells of the majestic surroundings. It took a little getting used to but then it was wonderful. After a few nights our senses opened more and more, taking in more and more, and our enjoyment increased more and more.

Next time I'll ditch my watch.

In one of Woody Allen's films he's sitting on a park bench with his girlfriend observing and conjecturing about the people walking by. His comments are both insightful and funny. He, for instance, would point out a man wearing a dark suit and dark glasses and venture he's a character from the *Godfather* movies.

In graduate social work school, one of our assignments was to sit outside and observe someone from a distance; writing our observations. It's a fascinating experience: scrutinizing everyday behavior. The professor and we students frequently laughed as these observations were read aloud in class.

While on the golf course with other golfers, I have occasionally commented on the beautiful sky. The comment doesn't get much response. The others are too engrossed with their games to think about the beauty of the natural world around them. A dinosaur could lumber by and it would draw scant attention, unless of course it interfered with their shot.

Take time each day to both see and observe. Marge and I were waiting for a plane when I decided to put down my book and watch some of the people around me. I saw a young man and the woman with him, who I took to be his mother. Our plane landed, and later in the day Marge and I were walking down the street where my son and his family live. I noticed a woman walking on the other side and recognized her as the woman I watched at the airport. I asked her if she had flown in from Detroit that morning. She was the same woman. We had a delightful conversation. This wouldn't have happened if not for the few moments I spent observing a few of the passengers around me at the airport.

I have seen a number of very entertaining YouTube videos where a group of accomplished singers suddenly appear in a crowded area, usually a shopping mall or train terminal, singing a delightful song. One of the things I find interesting about these videos is the number of people who don't take a few minutes to stop and listen to the wonderful performance. What could be more important than enjoying this serendipitous moment?

To those rushers, it is a beautiful moment that won't happen again.

Joshua Bell is a world renowned violinist. He once performed for about an hour incognito and for free in a New York City subway station. Everyone ignored him except a youngster who picked up on the exquisite music and stopped to listen.

Don't keep walking or talking when these special moments occur. Stop and take them in, for they are precious. Look for and embrace these precious moments.

Say to yourself, "This is special."

Learn to saunter and savor. Kenneth Grahame, author of "The Wind in the Willows," describes this lost art:

Nothing seems really to matter, that's the charm of it. Whether you get away, or whether you don't; whether you arrive at your destination or whether you reach somewhere else, or whether you never get anywhere at all, you're always busy, and you never do anything in particular; and when you've done it there's always something else to do, and you can do if you like, but you'd much better not.

When I read this quote to Marge she exclaimed, "That's you."

Spend time every now and then sauntering and savoring. See what comes your way and then do it, unless of course something else comes your way and then you may want to do that, but then you might not. That's the charm of it.

Almost all Americans suffer from a bad case of Calvinitis: after the puritanical Protestant theologian and reformer, John Calvin, who extolled the value of work. The thought of doing nothing sends people into a panic. Create empty spaces in your life. You will be amazed at how wonderfully the vacuums fill up.

Humility Opens Minds:

It was such an unusual experience that my friend Mike was eager to tell me about it. He said he was at a banquet and sat next to a professor from the University of Pennsylvania. Mike described him as a bona fide intellectual with an impressive resume of academic credentials, professional achievements and honors.

If anyone could bask in his own glory, it was this professor. Yet he spent the whole time querying Mike on every facet of his work. He obviously viewed Mike as an opportunity to learn something.

When you interact with others, you have a choice. You can be interesting or you can be interested. People who choose to be interesting are on stage having to be witty, entertaining and clever. People who are interested display a genuine interest in other people, asking open-ended questions followed by clarifying comments.

Interesting people may be popular, but interested people are loved.

Interested people quickly break down communication barriers.

I once told a Democrat friend of ours that Marge and I watched the 2012 Republican presidential debates. He asked me why we did that, knowing that Marge and I tend to vote Democrat. I told him that we wanted to better understand the Republican view on various national issues. He said he already knew where they stood and didn't need to hear it again.

He thinks he understands the Republican position: I wonder if he truly does. He certainly didn't want to hear anything that would challenge his negative views of Republicans. Perish the thought that he might agree with a candidate's position on an issue.

I'm sure die-hard Republicans display similar avoidance behavior.

A scientific friend of mine, knowing that I am a devout Christian, was surprised when I mentioned that I was reading a book written by an atheist scientist espousing a naturalistic explanation of the world, sans God. I told him that a naturalistic, evolutionary description of the world does not conflict with my Christian interpretation of creation, and that I read the book expecting to learn something, which I did.

My friend Mike, who takes a liberal view of Christianity, and I, who side with the conservatives, have often gone to the mat discussing our different perspectives. He once proposed we each read a book recommended by the other. He would recommend a book espousing liberal Christian views for me, and I would recommend a book espousing conservative

Christian views for him. We would then discuss these books.

I have learned much from our lively discussions, and as you will see when you come to the end of this book, he has greatly infused my thinking. I believe he feels the same about my influence on his thinking.

There was a TV show years ago where people of very different backgrounds and attitudes shared living quarters for a couple of months; an atheist with a Christian, a pro-choice activist with an abortion foe, a racist with an African-American, a Jew with an Arab.

Most of the participants benefited from the experience. While neither side drastically altered their views, they at least acknowledged each other's sincerity. They learned that few things are black-and-white, and that each position contains legitimate points. They stopped vilifying each other.

Years ago I read a column by a homosexual who attended an evangelical Christian gathering. He didn't hide his sexual identity. He was pleasantly surprised by the kind reception he received. Although he continued to challenge their position on homosexuality, his attitude toward them was far less harsh.

I have a friend who frequently pans Detroit; while I, on the other hand, speak positively of my hometown. Hoping to soften his attitude, I proposed that he and I attend a Sunday African-American church service in Detroit, which we did. The experience was exhilarating. In fact, the afterglow remained with me, and I believe him, for days. Mission accomplished!

We now plan on taking bus rides through the city.

Marge and I used to use an inner-city laundromat to wash and dry bedspreads. I always enjoyed the experience. The people we met there were usually reading their Bibles and gave us warm smiles and offers to help.

If only more people from the suburbs and the poor inner-cities occasionally worshipped or did their laundry together, there might be far less racial strife.

And finally, humility can prevent injustice.

I once asked an assistant prosecutor whether she feared her office would convict an innocent person. She confidently said this wouldn't happen because the office is staffed with highly competent and professional lawyers.

I thought afterward: As right as this answer sounds, it was the wrong answer. She should have said that this possibility worries her all the time, and she constantly reminds herself and her staff to be on the lookout for it.

To be forewarned is to be forearmed.

It isn't confidence that prevents an innocent person from going to jail, it's humility.

Humility Opens Hearts:

Neil Diamond sings a popular country-western song titled, *Husbands and Wives*. The lyrics include:

The angry word spoken in haste ... what a waste ... of two lives.

It's my belief ... pride is the chief cause ... in the decline ... in the number of husbands and wives.

Unkind words are spoken and hurt feelings remain, and remain, and remain.

The three most important words said in any relationship after "I love you" are "I was wrong" or "I am sorry."

I recall three occasions where friends told me about conflicts they were having with family members or other people. Each time I advised them to apologize to the other person for their behavior. You would have thought I had suggested they jump in Lake Michigan in January. They bristled at the very idea. One friend snapped, "My apologies don't come that easily." I suspect his apologies don't come at all. Another one, who is a devout Christian, told me reaching out to the other person and apologizing would *not* be the Christian thing to do. The third person made a half-hearted apology via e-mail.

I have had a chronic case of foot-in-the-mouth disease. I have said and done things that have hurt others. I strive to practice what I preach by quickly and sincerely apologizing to the offended person. I am thankful to those persons who have accepted my apologies. To those who haven't, I don't worry about it. I have done what is required of me. It's over.

Dave and Diane, the feuding couple, said a lot of things to each other during their counseling sessions, but I don't remember either of them saying, "You are right, I was wrong. I'm very sorry." Even better: "How can I change my behavior in order to make you happy?" What a positive difference in their marriage these words would have made.

Twelve-step programs, such as AA, have been shown to be highly effective in treating any number of addictions, such as, to alcohol, drugs and gambling. Their success is due in large part to humility: When group members openly state that they can't control their lives because of their addictions.

In many traditional Christian services, congregants make a general confession, stating, "I have not loved God with my whole heart, my whole soul and my whole mind, and I have not loved my neighbor as myself."

These humble statements act as a vaccine against the pernicious germs of egotism, pretensions and arrogance, and open the way for healing.

Humility not only heals, it can also be the doorway to very interesting worlds.

I volunteered for years at a Sunday soup kitchen that my church hosted three or four times a year. I liked the door duty where I controlled the flow. It was a great opportunity to talk with the guests. The more I interacted with them, the more I realized how little separated us. In fact I came to admire their patience, endurance and great spiritual strength. They opened my heart.

I once attended a Christian renewal weekend. I noticed one participant who I dismissed as a rube with his rumpled appearance and southern drawl. He later addressed the group and it turned out he was a psychiatrist in charge of all the State of Michigan mental health services.

Years ago I had lunch with a fellow church member who I didn't know very well. I thought it would be a tedious experience as this person seemed rather nondescript. We had a delightful conversation as he spoke about his years in New York City as a jazz musician.

One of my sisters and her husband, Ken, recently visited with Marge and me. Ken had a stroke years ago which impaired his mobility and speech. As a consequence I have tended in the past to keep my conversations with him brief. But on this visit I spent a fair amount of time with him which resulted in longer conversations. I discovered that although his speech is impaired, what he says is very interesting and funny. In fact, his humorous comments kept cracking me up.

My friend Emery told me about an experience when a draftsperson where he worked approached him because he knew Emery taught mathematics. He explained to Emery that he studies mathematics and builds violins as hobbies. Emery was amazed at the depth of his knowledge of math. He never would have guessed that this inconspicuous person possessed such sophisticated interests, knowledge and skills.

In these situations I and others were convinced we knew another person or a group of people, only to be proven wrong. Humility starts with realizing, or at least suspecting, that our perceptions of others may be wrong. In fact, we should assume we are wrong, and then seek to know who they really are.

We need to continually discover and rediscover people.

Marge and I have a "friend" who I don't like very much. There is always tension in the air when we're together. What if I changed my attitude at these times? Instead of tensing up and expecting friction between us, maybe I should try to better understand her by actively listening to her. I might find that she's wrestling with some huge problems, or we have much more in common than I think. My attitude toward her might change from anger to understanding, even admiration. The more you know a person, the more difficult it is to dislike them.

There's a Calvin and Hobbes cartoon where Calvin is digging a hole in the ground. Hobbes, his pretend tiger friend, asks what he has found. Calvin says, "A few dirty rocks, a weird root, and some disgusting grubs." Hobbes marvels, "On your first try?" Whereupon Calvin exclaims, "There's treasure everywhere."

When I'm in situations not to my liking, I remind myself that treasures await me there if I open my heart to them. For there are indeed treasures everywhere. You just need to be humble, i.e. flexible, enough to see and enjoy them. They are usually right under our noses.

I can't tell you how many times I've gone into situations kicking-and-screaming and came out of them smiling from ear-to-ear. On such occasions Marge will ask, "Now didn't you have a good time?" I answer, "Yes, I did."

Humility Opens Our Souls:

Mankind took a giant step forward in understanding the physical world through the Copernican

Revolution. Copernicus, along with Galileo, opened the eyes of the world when they proved that the sun does not revolve around the earth, but rather the earth revolves around the sun. We are not the center of the Universe; at least not astronomically.

Each of us needs to have a personal Copernican Revolution. We need to realize that we are not the center of the world: We are, instead, a part of something much bigger than ourselves. And by doing our individual part well, we are contributing to a greater good.

I, for instance, desired a speedy and outstanding success for my previous book. I was disappointed when this didn't happen. But what if an angel appeared to me and gave me a choice between modest success for my book, or no overt success but it would be read by someone who would be inspired to do something very beneficial for humanity. That someone could be either of my children, one of my grandchildren, some distant family relative, or someone completely unknown and unconnected to me. In other words, my book would be part of something greater. Which would I choose? I would choose being part of the greater good, which is the role I believe all of us play in life.

When I lamented the lack of acclaim for my book, my sister Florence wrote this to me: "If it touches some, helps some, your efforts will be worth it. When you go to heaven, those helped by your books will be lined up to thank you. Some of them you will know but most you won't. These people, unknown to you now, will tell you how, in some way, at some point in their lives, your words helped them. It will be a great day for you and for them."

I have a dear friend who sought a career in country-western music some years ago. He wrote, produced and sang an excellent CD of songs which didn't go very far. I believe his CD, and all the effort that went into it, is being honored beyond his wildest dreams in a place that is beyond his wildest dreams.

I now realize that every creative act, every act of kindness, love, courage, patience, etc. that humans perform have eternal significance. Knowing that significance is generally not available to us mortals, but it will eventually be revealed.

As Florence said, all will be revealed, in time, where there is no time.

I recall some particularly memorable times in my life when I adventurously opened my eyes, ears, heart and mind to the world around me.

They were during my college sophomore summer when I hitchhiked from Buffalo to Salt Lake City and back, and during my college junior year when I flew into London and returned home from Paris thirteen weeks later. I carried a small bag of clothes each time. I had a Youth Hostel card and directory while in England, Ireland and Europe, and lived on $3.50

per day. In America I had about $5 a day and no set sleeping plans.

I had a general itinerary but the plan was to stand on the side of the road, stick out my thumb and see where the winds blew me.

Wherever I ended up, I explored, usually by walking.

In America I visited the Grand Canyon and Bryce National Park with my sister and her Catholic missionary friends, I knocked around Chicago with a fellow traveler, and I looked in amazement as I stood on the side of the road in some Western state and watched a herd of wild horses gallop by.

In England, Ireland and Europe I walked through plenty of museums, toured ancient cities on foot, stood on a cliff overlooking the North Sea at the northernmost tip of Scotland, hit Munich beer halls with another traveler from Kansas, crossed over at Checkpoint Charlie and walked the streets of a still war-ravished East Berlin, strolled virtually alone through the incredible Pergamon Museum in East Berlin, stood in a gas chamber in a former German concentration camp, lounged for days at an Italian youth hostel on the Mediterranean, and walked with awe through St. Peter's Basilica and the Vatican, the center of my childhood Catholic faith.

I totally opened myself up to the world — drivers who picked me up, strangers who helped direct my steps, lovely people who opened their homes to me for an evening, fellow travelers with whom we shared stories and advice; cities of all sizes and countrysides that provided delights at every turn.

I continue this same humble reliance "on the kindness of strangers" today, albeit on a smaller scale.

Whenever I'm grappling with a problem, be it as simple as a recipe or directions, or as complicated as investment decisions or parenting advice, I like to put on my "Ah shucks, I don't know; what would you do?" hat. People love to give advice and someone usually has the right answer. I consider all of the responses and then implement one. I also like to tell the winners how well their advice served me, which always pleases them.

This book may not have been written if not for two questions I posed to people: "What, when you think about it, keeps you humble?" and "Tell me about an important love experience in your life and how did it impact you?" The answers shaped much of my thinking contained in this book.

To paraphrase Thomas Edison, who said, "Genius is one percent inspiration and ninety-nine percent perspiration:" *Genius, to my mind, is one percent inspiration and ninety-nine percent asking good questions and hearing the answers.*

Finally, humility is sometimes thrust upon us, with surprisingly happy results.

Years ago a friend told me about his business partner, who he described as being fiercely competitive, driven and combative. The partner had a neurological collapse which left him immobile and helpless. In that humble state his combative personality disappeared and was replaced with tranquility and kindness. As his strength and mobility returned, sadly his former combatant self also returned.

Growing old, which is the most humbling of experiences, can also be an enlightening and enriching time of life, offering opportunities to garner riches and joys that are frequently overlooked when youthful strength and arrogance prevail.

As my mortal clock winds down, I find I am less driven by social expectations and am more inclined to pursuit personal interests. I socialize less, read and study more, and, as evidenced by my books, reflect on the content and meaning of life. My only regret is that few people display my passion for "being Greek," so it's a lonely adventure at times.

Humility may indeed open the windows of the world to us, but what role does it play in transforming an ordinary person into "a somebody?"

To answer this crucial question, let us first look at some of the popular means people use to distinguish themselves.

Let's start with something my sister Florence pointed out years ago when she said, "Joe, if anyone was born under a lucky star it was you."

I had to agree with her.

Some people are born on third base with high IQs and/or family wealth and connections. Well, I wasn't born on third base, but I've hit a lot of triples in my life with my eyes closed.

As a boy I enjoyed watching the TV comedy show, "You'll Never Get Rich." It starred Phil Silvers as Sergeant Bilko, a fast-talking hustler. I remember one episode where Bilko is having a lucky day but doesn't realize it. The show starts with the soldiers shivering in a cold shower till Bilko steps in and the water suddenly turns hot and comfortable. These serendipitous moments continue throughout the day for the uncomprehending Bilko. The other soldiers in his company catch on and tell him. Bilko realizes he is having a lucky day and races to place a bet before midnight. He bets on a long-shot horse and listens to the race over the radio. The horse takes a big lead and as it nears the finish line the clock strikes midnight and the horse fades and loses the race.

Of all the episodes of this show I watched, why does this one stick in my memory? I think it's because it struck a chord with me. I realized on a subconscious level that I too am living a lifetime of lucky days, months and years.

— I failed the second grade and barely got out of the seventh grade in elementary school, yet nothing gives me more pleasure than reading and learning.

— I failed the N.Y. State Regency exam in English in my high school junior year and barely passed it in my senior year, yet I have written two fairly literate books.

— I obsessively played basketball as a teen and all I had to show for it was warming the bench in my high school junior year, yet the team I played with won the Catholic High School Basketball Championship that year.

— I didn't have the college grades to get into graduate psychology school and therefore into the mental health field which was my dream, yet I earned a Master of Social Work degree and did mental health counseling for almost four decades.

— I played a relatively unimportant role at the HMO I worked for, yet that company pioneered providing pre-paid outpatient and inpatient medical services to a Medicaid population and was financially very successful.

— I can be abrasive and say a lot of stupid things, yet I have had a number of wonderful friendships and my brothers and sisters never stop loving me.

— (This one is important.) I was so shy in high school and college I could hardly get a date and when I did they didn't turn out well, yet I ended up in a wonderful marriage with an absolute gem of a woman.

— I spent more time playing tennis and jogging when I should have been with my children, yet our two children turned out to be remarkable individuals.

— (This one blows me away.) Marge and I had social work careers, which are notoriously poor paying, yet we have a very comfortable retirement and are in a position to help our children and grandchildren, if needed.

— I have always driven old cars and spend very little money on myself, yet it gives me great pleasure picking up restaurant tabs and donating to charities.

— I've sat on only one board of directors, for a nursing home. My contribution was minimal, yet it constructed a beautiful extended care senior citizen community during my tenure.

None of these wonderful things should have happened but they did. Is it that lucky star my sister said I was born under?

Luck has two divergent definitions: Being at the right place at the right time; and, When preparation meets opportunity.

To me it's not the presence of luck that's important, but rather what it spawns. It's a question of how grateful we are for our good fortune. I know lots of people who are up to their ears in whipped cream and are ungrateful, while I know others who rarely catch a break in life yet are full of gratitude. Many of the latter are African-Americans who are struggling to make ends meet yet are always thanking Jesus.

Isaac Bashevis Singer, the Jewish Nobel Laureate in Literature, once said that he thanks God for every word he writes. I am thankful every winter morning when I awake in a warm house, when I have a nourishing meal, and when I enjoy the company of family and friends. I am keenly aware that the winds of fate could have easily blown differently in my life.

I learned this *Attitude of Gratitude* from my parents. My father always reminded his children to be grateful for everything we had, which often wasn't much. I once watched a news show with my elderly mother that reported on a rather contemptible individual. I thought she would condemn him as I was doing. She instead said, "Aren't you glad you didn't turn out like him."

I abhor the attitude that is so prevalent these days that, "I'm a self-made man (woman) and I deserve everything I have." Translated: "I've got mine, screw you." Or, "I'm in the rescue boat, pull up the ladder."

A grateful heart invariably leads to a compassionate and generous one. Yet, sadly, humans are egotists who far too often take blessings for granted and use them to lord over others. It is one of the ugliest things humans do. Rather than transforming us from an ordinary person into "a somebody," these blessings oftentimes make us proud, selfish and mean.

The answer must lie elsewhere.

There's the existentialist proposition that says the meaning of our lives is determined by the good we bring into the world. So it's not a question of whether we're average or not, it's how many people have benefited from our presence on Earth.

It's tempting to get into this kind of moral accounting but I don't think it's wise.

I know I have helped a lot of people: That was the purpose of my work as a psychiatric counselor.

I had a Jewish client who said I was a mensch. Mensch is Yiddish for "a good person." Another client told me that I was the nicest person she has ever known.

I have always tried to be a good person throughout my life, but I'm a realist enough to know that I fall far short of this goal.

I can't recall ever deliberately mistreating anyone, but I suspect I have hurt any number of persons by not listening to them when I should have, by displaying negative body language toward them, by failing to be helpful; and through gossip, backbiting and other human devices that intentionally or unintentionally harm others.

I hold on to slights and feel a satisfaction when those individuals who have slighted me have problems. I'm also competitive and secretly agree with Oscar Wilde who said, "It's not enough that I succeed, my friends must fail."

If such a moral inventory was taken of me, I don't know which side of the ledger I would fall under. Probably the wrong side.

I wonder how anyone would fare. I recall a preacher who said we come into the world 98% self-centered. If we work really hard at it, we might leave the world 94% self-centered.

You can't be self-centered and loving at the same time, for love means to be more focused on another than on yourself.

So do good deeds transform life out of the ordinary into the extraordinary? It's wonderful and highly advisable that humans do nice things for others, but almost all of the saints the world has known were well aware of their shortcomings. Mother Teresa reportedly confessed her sins once a week.

My sister Florence is one of the kindest persons to walk this earth. She has been recognized a number of times for her humanitarian deeds. I was surprised by her response when I asked her what keeps her humble. She quoted Psalms 51:3 "For I know my transgressions, and my sin is ever before me."

It seems the more saintly people are, the more aware they are of their failings.

The answer must lie elsewhere.

Maybe the TV evangelist and best-selling author Joel Osteen and his Prosperity Gospel have the answer.

This position, which is extremely popular and which makes a ton of money for its proselytizers, holds that we are what we believe, so set those beliefs high. This take on Holy Scripture informs us that we are made in the image and likeness of God and that God doesn't make junk. In fact, we are created for greatness. All people have to do is claim their greatness and good things will follow.

There are holes in this philosophy big enough to drive a truck through.

Osteen, who professes to being a Christian preacher and sprinkles Bible quotes throughout his presentations, fails to mention humankind's fallen nature. Our propensities, for instance, to seek success at the expense of others. To scheme and connive to get ahead. We might be reaching for the stars by day but we frequently wallow in the gutters by night. Behind almost every great fortune is a sin or a crime.

How would you, I or anyone behave if we thought we could get away with something? I suspect temptation would eventually get the better of most of us. People quickly contest a billing mistake when it costs them, but don't when the mistake costs the company. They never fail to come up with a good rationalization for their cheating.

It is also questionable that believing is achieving. I can talk myself into running a marathon but that doesn't mean I can do it. In fact, such positive thinking may be setting me up for failure, disappointment and unwillingness to try again.

And is it useful to go through life with a Pollyanna view of the world; thinking goodness surrounds us?

At the start of my career my boss made this comment. "Joe, you expect too much from people. When they don't meet your expectations, you become disappointed and even bitter. I, on the other hand, don't expect much from others and rarely become upset with them."

Americans are probably the most optimistic people in the world. Optimism is practically our national credo. Yet research has shown that pessimistic people live happier and healthier lives. Researchers conjecture that a healthy dose of pessimism puts people on guard for health and other problems, and they then take the necessary actions to prevent them. And as mystery writer Rex Stout once said, "A pessimist gets nothing but pleasant surprises."

Con artists are looking for trusting, optimistic and greedy individuals. After being fleeced out of their life savings, most of these victims remarked on how nice the con artist was. How much they trusted him or her. "Con" stands for confidence. These gullible people (i.e., suckers) had confidence in the crooks. Appearing friendly and nice are the con artist's stock in trade.

When it comes to making most business, and particularly investment decisions, I heed the advice of Machiavelli who wrote in *The Prince* that humans are fickle, hypocritical, greedy and deceitful. Starting from this premise has spared me a lot of misery and has made me a lot of money.

Marge tells me my view of people is too negative. She's probably right. I will jokingly say that I make John Calvin, who viewed humans as totally depraved, look like a cockeyed optimist.

That's an overstatement of my view of humanity. I like Woody Allen's comment that the world is totally messed up, but it's the only place you can get a good pastrami sandwich. I put it this way: Human beings, including myself, are totally screwed up, but it's nice having a beer or coffee with them.

G.K. Chesterton, the British novelist and Christian apologist, was walking down the street with a friend. The friend spotted someone he knew and said, "See that fellow over there: He's going places, because he believes in himself."

Chesterton responded, "Right to the insane asylum."

What I think Chesterton is saying with this severe comment is that people who live only within the confines of themselves and not for something larger are doomed to unhappiness.

Americans generally define themselves through their own individual achievements. Non-western societies, on the other hand, are more communal oriented: where individual success is secondary to the group's success.

Which is better for achieving individual happiness and group success? It's probably not an *either/or* answer.

Athletes strive for individual excellence, but usually say they much prefer a team championship to any individual honors. Teams full of superstars frequently don't live up to the group's potential. Team success is usually determined by a delicate balance between individual performances and team identify and cohesiveness.

But this issue aside, humans are fatally flawed. People blame con artists for fleecing them, but it's their greed that led them into the trap.

No. Believing in yourself and in others isn't the answer.

The answer must lie elsewhere.

There is a fourth and quite intriguing possibility: the evolutionary angle. Let's suppose that nature/ God played an interesting trick on humans. In order to advance societies, humans have implanted in their psyches the uncomfortable notion that they are average. Humans are then driven to prove that they're not average by performing the exceptional. We're a race of overachievers.

There's an adage in professional schools that A-students teach while B-students end up working for the C-students. It's not the brainiacs who make the world go round, it's the average students who want to show up the A & B-students.

Political humorist, P.J. O'Rourke, observed that many candidates are running for office, as he imagines one of them admitting, "in order to even the score with those grade-school classmates of mine who, thirty-five years ago, gave me the nickname Fish Face."

I wonder if the motivating force behind my writing two books is to disprove to myself and others the assertion that I'm average.

Show me someone who has something to prove and I'll show you a winner.

Maybe parents make a mistake by inflating their children's egos with endless praise. Limiting their expectations of them might work better in motivating them to excel: Implying that they can't do something might propel them to achieve it.

A friend of mine used to say that you never want to insult Joe's tennis game: He'll come at you like a tiger if you do. The way to beat him, he further advised, is to flatter his game.

I once had to replace our car radio/cassette player. I told my son, Chris, that I would buy a new system and have it installed. He was a high school student at the time with no automotive experience. He said he could install it. I doubted he could and told him so, but I reluctantly gave him the go-ahead. As he worked on it for about an hour, I was fairly certain that he was messing up the electronics in the car. To my amazement, he installed it perfectly.

I think he delighted in surprising me, which he certainly did. Both my children never stop surprising and impressing me with their achievements.

The flaw with thinking that achievement equals worth is that it may indeed motivate people to achieve great things but it does nothing for lasting happiness. Achievements based on proving ourself frequently leaves us feeling phony, empty and even cheated.

Woody Allen once said he has achieved everything he's set out in life to do, yet he feels he's gotten screwed.

All the achievements in the world won't dispel a nagging sense of inadequacy. Fame and accolades are fickle and fleeting, and frequently worsen self-doubts and insecurities. Davy Crockett said, "Fame is like a shaved pig with a greased tail, and it is only after it has slipped through the hands of some thousands, that some fellow, by mere chance, holds on to it."

Scratch the evolutionary argument for transforming humans from being ordinary into being "a somebody."

The answer must lie elsewhere.

Luck, doing nice things, believing in yourself and excelling certainly have value, and individually and/or collectively yield satisfying and commendable results, yet they come up short in the transformation process which changes ordinary humans into being "a somebody."

That answer, for me, came from my friend Mike Denomme. He and I have thrashed out all sorts of psychological, theological, political and philosophical issues over the decades. He keeps saying that they all come down to one thing: love.

I usually dismissed this contention as being simplistic. I now realize he's right.

Poets immortalize it, religions claim it, scientists try to study it, writers describe it, singers rhapsodize about it, everyone seeks it, some people die for it, and everyone grieves its loss. It's the force that has brought the world into creation, sustains it, has redeemed it, and makes living worthwhile. Yet ask people to define or describe love in their lives and they are frequently at a loss for words.

In the Foreword of this book Mike quotes the eminent theologian Karl Barth, who summarized his complex Christian theology in the words of the Sunday school song: "Jesus loves me, this I know, for the Bible tells me so." Mike then writes about an even greater thinker, Thomas Aquinas, who presumably had a taste of divine love and declared his towering works as "so much straw" when compared to experiencing God's love. In other words, love renders everything else in life meaningless.

This sentence can be edited to read: _____ loves me, this I know, for _____ tells me so. Each person can fill in the blanks.

My friend Sharon Denomme writes, "My parents, aunts, uncles, cousins, teachers, Brownie and Girl Scout leaders, Sunday school teachers, and church youth fellowship leaders all bathed me in love." At the age of 17 she was seriously hurt in an auto accident and spent three weeks in the hospital. She received cards and gifts from many people, some whom she hardly knew. She describes how these expressions of concern and love impacted her: "So many cards! So many messages! So much love! It was awesome!"

She continues, "The impact this had on me was to make me realize that I actually meant A LOT to MANY people ... It was very humbling to realize that I was someone who so many people cared so much about."

For Sharon the sentence reads: <u>Lots of people</u> love me, this I know, for <u>all those loving cards and messages</u> tell me so.

She was dazzled and humbled by this outpouring of love for her.

When individuals are given awards, they frequently say they are humbled by the honor. They mean it.

One of the most surprising and satisfying moments in my life was when I hosted a celebratory dinner for the trainers of a Staff-Patient Relations Improvement Program I had organized and coordinated. As I finished my few comments of thanks to the trainers and left the podium I received a standing ovation. I had absolutely no idea I was thought of so highly. Thinking of that moment still warms my heart.

People have little to no idea of how much they are loved. As my sister Florence says, much of that love will be revealed in heaven. While on earth we only have glimpses of it.

God's love for us is even more incomprehensible. As Simon and Garfunkel sing in their song, *Mrs. Robinson*:

And here's to you, Mrs. Robinson
Jesus loves you more than you will know ...

My friend Tina told me that as youngsters her son Damon would mercilessly taunt his sister Lyndsay. Yet when Valentine's Day came around Lyndsay gave Damon a Valentine honestly professing her love for him. Damon confessed to his mother that he couldn't understand how Lyndsay could love him, given how badly he treats her.

Tina responded, "Damon, welcome to the world of unconditional love." Love that is not deserved yet is freely given.

My friend Emery continues to be amazed that his wife, Dee, married him and continues to cherish his company. I truly can't understand why Marge and my six siblings seem to like me so much. I can be a royal pain in the butt. These are, or should be, the sentiments of every happily married person.

Love requires sacrifice. No sacrifice, no love. The greater the sacrifice, the greater the love. "Greater love has no one than this: to lay down one's life for one's friends." John 15:13

Decades ago I taught a class at Marygrove College, a small women's liberal arts college in Detroit. As I started my class I realized that I didn't have the class roster. I excused myself and rushed to the faculty office to get it. As I was racing down the hallway I glimpsed a crucifix that was hanging on the wall. Having been raised Catholic, I have seen hundreds of crucifixes so this one should not have stood out. Yet it did. I stopped, turned and stared at it. These words kept going through my mind: *He died because he loved me. He died because he loved me.*

I couldn't understand how someone could love me so much. It was both a baffling and wondrous feeling.

I gave considerable thought to the cover design for this book. I wanted an image that conveyed humility and love. The only one that came to mind was of an innocent person nailed to a cross out of love. I abandoned this idea and turned the manuscript and decision over to the artist, Erica Chappuis, who painted the cover design. She, as you can see, came to the same idea I originally had.

Love and humility go hand-in-hand. That's what makes love so wonderful: We feel we don't deserve it, and we don't.

As mentioned earlier, Marge and I once visited a number of national parks in the American Southwest. As I stood on one of the ridges of the Grand Canyon gazing at the multi-colored walls, I was speechless. I felt wonderfully insignificant in the presence of such majestic beauty.

I live in constant awe. How, I keep wondering, can each human face be so different and attractive when all there is to them are two eyes, a nose, a mouth, cheeks and a chin? How can each snowflake be perfectly designed and different? We're talking trillions of snowflakes, perhaps in just one huge snowfall. How, on Earth, can the Earth, and everything in the Universe, stay perfectly in place?

Albert Einstein said, "There are only two ways to live your life. One is as though nothing is a miracle. The other is as though everything is a miracle."

I live mostly in the latter world of miracles; accepting science while embracing the wonder of life.

Scientists, I'm sure, can reduce love to neurotransmitters and the like. Freud reduced God to a displaced father figure. Love, God, and most things in life are greater than — and transcend — scientific explanations.

That's what love feels like. It simply blows us away. It is awesome!

Love not only blows us away, it transforms us.

I had a friend, now deceased, who was married to a woman whom I, and others, found daffy.

My friend adored his wife. To him she was the personification of beauty and goodness.

Their daughter once tried to advise her mother not to act so flighty in company. My friend was baffled and upset by his daughter's comments. To him his wife was perfect in every way. For, indeed, she was perfect: His love for her made her perfect.

Barbra Streisand sings a song in the musical *Funny Girl* that has the lyric:

His love makes me beautiful, so beautiful, so beautiful ...

Love makes us beautiful, and special, and important, and needed, and every other lovely superlative found in the dictionary. It makes all of us "a somebody."

I, for instance, love Detroit. Where most people see squalor and ruin, I see courage, spiritual strength, compassion, love and hope. Like a true lover, I will defend Detroit against its detractors.

When I asked people about their experiences with love, the most frequent response was: "Love is knowing that person will always be there for me," or as one spouse put it, "Our job is to make each other happy."

My friend Mike's mother has been bedridden in a nursing home for about seven years. His mother's doctor said he has never seen a more caring family. Someone is by her side virtually every day. Mike said this is because their mother was always there for them throughout their lives, and now it is her children's great privilege to be by her side. As he writes, "No amount of loving attention to her now could possibly match the loving attention she was always giving us."

I had an African-American client named Thelma who lived a life of hardships and disappointments but was full of gratitude and was always thanking Jesus. I once asked her why she always thanked Jesus, as her life seems so difficult. She said, "Jesus has brought me this far, he will bring me home." She knew that Jesus would always be there for her.

Can we love people we don't like?

This brand of love is the mother lode of all love; and like any precious metal it isn't easy to get to.

You make a decision to love that person and you stand pat on that decision: To love that person "for better, for worse, for richer, for poorer, in sickness and in health ... till death us do part."

I had a former boss who had a stroke shortly after retiring. He once passed me over for promotion. I made a commitment to myself that I would stand by him in his hour of need. I visited him as much as I could while he lay in a nursing home bed for years. This commitment was nothing compared to his wife's, who was by his side virtually every day: keeping him company, cheering him up and advocating for him.

Interestingly, I was the one who stood by him, while the staff he promoted rarely, if ever, visited him.

Marge and I have had a minor feud with neighbors across the street over the constant parking of their S.U.V. in front of our house. They recently re-landscaped their front yard. I saw the wife and told her how beautiful the new landscaping looks and how much Marge and I enjoy seeing it. She seemed very pleased with the compliment.

We need also to remind ourselves that others have loved us when we have been less than lovable. We must do the same.

I must confess, I am not good at loving people I don't like. Truth be told: I'm not very good at loving people who I do like. I am, however, good at praying for people. I continually ask God to bless everyone I have known, particularly those individuals whom I have hurt in any way. God, you see, is much better at loving than I am.

I live a life full of material comforts, even excesses. Though I didn't intend it, these comforts are frequently paid for with a high price by many persons who work at grueling jobs, for grueling hours, for marginal pay. I owe them all a huge debt of gratitude, and an apology. They all deserve, and will receive, God's special blessings.

How does love move from being an act of the will to being an act of the heart; when loving acts spring naturally from a kinship with all of humanity?

Loving acts, as I just stated, generally begin as a decision and not as a feeling, but when repeated they become more natural responses; like an athlete who endlessly practices a skill till it becomes reflexive and natural. As it is said, "They work hard to make it look easy."

I have known a handful of people who seem to love naturally. I am in awe of them. The rest of us need to heed the AA adage: *Fake it till you make it.* This makes our loving acts even more impressive because they don't come natural and easy.

I think one of the most wondrous things about love is that death can't destroy it. I knew a very fine person who lost his young son to suicide. He said the experience nearly cost him his sanity. What saved him was reading the book, *Heaven,* by Randy Alcorn. The author makes a scriptural case for the existence and makeup of heaven. The book quotes such scriptural passages as Revelation 21:4, "He will wipe every tear from their eyes. There will be no more death or mourning or crying or pain, for the old order of things has passed away."

He told me he now realizes the loss of his son is temporary, for their love for each other will resume in a place where love can never again be lost: a place called heaven. His sorrow continues but there is now eager anticipation.

Love gets even more incomprehensible, and amazing.

In the book *Why does the World Exist?: An Existential Detective Story*, author Jim Holt confronts the riddle — How can something come from nothing? He interviewed a number of eminent thinkers who proposed various scientific and philosophical explanations, all of which come up short.

None of them, as I recall, proposed this answer — Love.

The author should have interviewed my friend Rev. Greg Sammons. I once asked Greg what keeps him humble. He said, "Humility is being connected to the earth, and it is a good thing: not to think we are nothing, not to think we are everything, but to think of ourselves as the dust God picked up and made capable through his grace of receiving his gift of Everlasting Life."

Love transforms the insignificant into the significant. And what can be more insignificant than nothing, and what can be more significant than eternal life. That is the power of Divine Love.

Just as the human eye and ear can detect only a small range of sights and sounds in the light and sound spectrums, human understanding is equally limited in the love spectrum.

Fr. Steven Kelly celebrates a Eucharist service at our church most days of the week, where few attend on weekdays to over a hundred on Sundays. He celebrates each service with the same degree of solemnity and devoutness regardless of the attendance. On weekdays there may be only a few people in the pews, but who's to say the church isn't packed to the rafters with the faithful worshipping God in a heavenly realm. Who's to say my friend's country-western CD isn't delighting a countless number of listeners in a place of pure love unseen by human eyes. Or that the works and deeds of every creative and loving person aren't being enjoyed and honored by a multitude of cheering fans in the place where all creative and loving acts are celebrated.

It's a place where all lost dreams come true, beyond a person's wildest expectations.

This isn't pie-in-the-sky thinking; it has an impressive intellectual pedigree.

Plato spoke of such a place in his "Allegory of the Cave," where knowledge of this world is limited to mere shadows emanating from a realm of perfect reality and truth. Hamlet put it this way to Horatio, "There are more things in heaven and earth ... than are dreamt of in your philosophy." And St. Paul makes it a trifecta: "For now we see through a glass, darkly, but then face to face; now I know in part; but then shall I know even as I am known." 1Cr. 13-12 KJV

The Beatles bridge the chasm between the imperfect and perfect worlds in their song, *All You Need Is Love:*

Nothing you can do that can't be done.
Nothing you can sing that can't be sung.
Love, in other words, makes all things possible.

My friend Mike had a spiritual director years ago who would say to him, "Mike, can't you feel the love?"

I've attended a number of Bible studies over the years. I feel many of these classes miss seeing the forest because of the trees, as the full force of God's love for us doesn't always come through. I, for instance, recently listened to a lecture on the Book of Genesis where the lecturer made the following points:

— God shows his grace with warnings and corrections.
— God shows his grace in guiding our lives.
— God shows his grace in never leaving us.
— God shows his grace in his eternal plan.

The instructor defined grace as unmerited favor. Why, I thought, use the somewhat confusing term of grace when he should have said:

— God shows his <u>love for us</u> with warnings and corrections.
— God shows his <u>love for us</u> in guiding our lives.
— God shows his <u>love for us</u> in never leaving us.
— God shows his <u>love for us</u> in his eternal plan.

We learned about Jacob and his family. The message, to me, is simple: Jacob and his family were totally screwed up, yet God loved each of them and made a way for their success and happiness. He continues to love every screwed-up individual and family (which is all of us), and is making a way for our success and happiness.

The Bible is a compilation of love letters to us. You read the Bible not so much to understand it but "to feel the love."

Years ago I asked our neighbor to join Marge and me for Sunday service. His response caught me off guard. He asked why he should go. I gave him some lame answer about it being beneficial for his children.

I have posed this question to a few church-going Christians. Almost all of them fail to provide a very good answer. I've thought to myself: How can Christians expect to get nonbelievers to attend church if they can't articulate why they go?

My answer now to that question is this: God loves me. I love God. I and others celebrate that loving relationship each Sunday in church. Sunday worship at African-American churches absolutely explode with this celebration of love.

God's love is the Hound of Heaven. You can run and hide from it but it will eventually capture and enrapture you. And when it does you will truly wonder why you fought it for so long.

Louis Armstrong's song, *What a Wonderful World*, says it all. The lyrics go like this:

I see friends shaking hands ... sayin' ... how do you do

They're really sayin' ... I love you

Marge and I took a trip to Hawaii in 2011. Honeymooners were everywhere. I enjoyed the scenic beauty but I was captivated even more by the love the starry-eyed lovers had for each other. Their love cast an enchanting spell. They loved everything about the other person.

I knocked Joel Osteen earlier in this book but Joel Osteen affirms people in a big way. He reminds them that they are precious and special in the eyes of God, which are the eyes of love. People walk out of his sermons feeling special and loved.

His theology might be shaky but his message is straight from heaven.

My sister Florence is one of the most affirming persons I know. When I told her of this book, she said that I should change the title from *Joe's Gift* to *Joe's a Gift ... To us all*.

My friend Mike is equally affirming. When I ask Mike to review something I've written, he usually responds by first stating that's it's second only to Shakespeare in quality. That is certainly a hyperbole, but the sentiment is genuine. To his loving heart, the point of the manuscript is not to ascertain its literary qualities, but rather to affirm me as a person.

I strive to affirm everyone I meet. I once worried that I might be crossing a line by telling women that they look beautiful or on complimenting them on their attire. A female friend of mine reassured me: "Joe, don't worry about it. Everyone loves a compliment."

I have been in a Bible study program for the past two years. Each year I'm part of a group of about ten men who discuss biblical passages. I made a decision to tell each group member how thankful I am that they are in the group, as I appreciate their insightful, humorous or humble answers and comments. Each member brings something special to the group and I try to honor their contributions.

I know it is very difficult for many people to pay a compliment. I remember a reader of my other book walking by me, with his head down and whispering, "Nice book." I was very thankful he got the compliment out.

Affirming others is a wonderful way of saying, I love you.

Love happens right under our noses but is often missed.

The Episcopal church Marge and I attend is in downtown Detroit. Occasionally street people will stray into one of the services. These people frequently have histories of alcohol and drug abuse. A few are not in their right mind as they have significant thought disorders.

One Sunday, such a person came in and sat in one of the pews. He was disheveled and dirty. He was talking to himself but not loud enough to disrupt the service. The ushers were keeping a close eye on him.

He was the type of person "normal" people avoid by not making eye contact and staying distant.

At the Communion a young parishioner went up to him, touched his arm and invited him to the Communion rail for at least a blessing. She escorted him there and back to his seat. After the service she took him down to the coffee hour, gave him refreshments, and kindly listened to his deluded notions for about thirty minutes.

I asked a few parishioners afterwards if they noticed anything unusual that morning. They all said they hadn't. I mentioned this incident, commenting what a great act of love it was. Then they saw it.

My friend Paul said he was singularly inept at sports in junior high school, and there was a cruel classmate who kept reminding him of his ineptitude. He recalls running a mile with classmates and lagging far behind. One of the other runners, who had finished the mile, noticed Paul struggling, ran beside him, and coaxed him to the finish line.

In the first instance the parishioner was saying to the derelict, **I love you**, and in the second instance the helpful classmate was saying to Paul, **I love you.**

Life is full of these **I love you** cards and messages. Marge keeps my clothes clean and neat and prepares great meals for me. I go shopping and watch TV mystery shows with her even though I generally dislike doing these things. My family calls to talk or takes the time to visit. My friend Dick invites me to golf with him even though he shoots in the seventies and eighties while I stink up the course with my game. Friends in our poker club buy a certain kind of beer for me because they know I like it. A friend says he is sorry for anything he may have said or done in the past that might have hurt me. The neighbor who is always helpful when I have mechanical problems. Anybody who gives me a smile. Anyone who asks, "How are you doing?" and is eager to listen. Anyone who brings up in conversation something that is on my mind or heart. Every volunteer activity.

The list goes on and on: Entertainers who delight us; physicians and surgeons who heal us; athletes who excite us; garbage collectors who take our trash; preachers who inform us; politicians who serve us; the young man who keeps my lawn and shrubs looking great; writers and journalists who enlighten and delight us; police officers who protect us; spouses or partners who have sex even though they aren't in the mood; men who open and close car doors for women; dinner guests who gladly eat whatever the hosts serve even though they don't like it and then compliment them on their culinary feast ... They are all saying, whether they know it or not, **I love you**.

I once noticed a note taped to the desk of the department office manager where I worked that read: "Lord, let me be a blessing to someone today." It could have easily read: "Lord, let me give an **I Love You** message to someone today."

Everyone should start their day intent on giving **I Love You** messages to others.

I worked for a company whose medical director ended all staff meetings with the enjoinder: "Be kind to the patient." Companies would be wise to always remind their staff that everything they do should say, **I love you**. The work environment and profitability will most likely soar.

Every beautiful thing in nature also sings the same refrain: **I love you**.

This book isn't worth the paper it's printed on or the electrons on the screen if it doesn't say to its readers: **I love you**.

And here's one of the most marvelous things about giving a gift of love to someone: We are giving that same gift to ourselves.

Marge sometimes gets down on me for giving panhandlers money. I tell her that I am giving a gift to myself. "Did you see the joy on his face," I gladly exclaim. That joyful look has paid me back in full.

She, however, tells me she gets much more pleasure from giving gifts than in receiving them.

The love we give has wonderful ways of returning to us tenfold and more.

Gifts of love are exchanged between people every moment of every day: Each precious one says, **I love you**.

And here's the really fun part. These gifts are like Easter eggs — they are both out in the open and half-hidden at the same time. You have to keep your eyes open to see them. They're easy to find. Look around and you will see loving acts. Soon you will feel as I did in Hawaii: *Love is everywhere!*

Marge and I attended the celebration of her sister and brother-in-law's 50th wedding anniversary. The weekend was a festival of love; from the family members who traveled from near and far to be there, to the daughter and daughter-in-law who superbly arranged everything, to the family's concern for the son/brother and his wife who couldn't attend due to a serious medical problem, to the toasts made at the celebration dinner to the couple's lifelong commitment of love to each other.

It wasn't hard to find **I love you** eggs that weekend; they were everywhere.

I should be careful not to paint too rosy a picture here. I spent decades counseling hundreds of depressed patients who, try as they might, couldn't see a single love message around them. Telling them they are there wouldn't help them; in fact, it could worsen their depression.

I sometimes think I would like to send beautiful bouquets to strangers around the country with the message: *From someone who loved you a long time ago*. I'm sure they would cherish those flowers for the feeling that at least one person has loved them in their life. Those flowers and that realization could help them in getting through the rough patches.

I chose this cover design because it shouts: **I love you!**

My friend Sharon occasionally takes out the box of cards she received decades ago while recovering from her injuries, and joyfully reads them. I have a note Marge wrote to me years ago when I was out of work which I keep in my wallet. I read it every now and then, and it always lifts my spirits. It says: GOOD LUCK. REMEMBER, I LOVE YOU!

That's *Joe Gift*, and everyone's gift. It's the love we receive and give. It's the love that abounds in and throughout the world.

It's a gift that comes in all shapes, sizes and colors; wrapped in God's love which is the fountainhead of all love.

A little girl asked her mother what color is Jesus. As the mother searched for an answer, these words came forth: "What color is love?"

As we open and reopen these countless gifts, we echo Sharon's joy:

"So many (**I love you**) cards! So many (**I love you**) messages! So much love! It is awesome!"

It's a gift that says: <u>Love makes everybody "a somebody."</u> That includes people who are average in everything they do. Like me.

THE SECRET TO LIVING A MORE FULFILLED LIFE

by

JOSEPH ALFF, M.S.W.

The *Secret to Living a More Fulfilled Life* is a fascinating and groundbreaking book that turns the conventional thinking of what constitutes a happy and successful life on its head. Joseph Alff, M.S.W., drawing on forty years as a psychiatric counselor, skillfully unravels the most perplexing prescription for achieving human fulfillment ever offered: That those who exalt themselves will be humbled and those who humble themselves will be exalted. Using vignettes based on personal and professional experiences, he explains that a person's natural response to the inherent struggles of human existence (humans against nature, others, self, evil, and even God) is for self-glorification, which is a hollow victory that robs individuals of fulfilling relationships and rich life experiences. He offers an alternative approach to living based on belief in oneself, tempered with contrition and humility. This refocuses us from ourselves to others, ushering in the quality of life we desire.

177 pages

CPSIA information can be obtained at www.ICGtesting.com
Printed in the USA
BVOW03s1111190813

328905BV00006B/15/P